THIS BOOK BELONGS TO

DEDICATION

This Garden Journal is dedicated to all gardeners who want to plan, organize, and track their planting schedule, plant health, and gardens throughout the year.

You are my inspiration for producing this book and I'm honored to be a part of helping you manage and retain important information regarding your garden.

HOW TO USE THIS BOOK

This Gardening Log Book will help you record, collect, and organize your information in an easy to use format.

Here are examples of information for you to fill in and write the details of your garden.

Fill in the following information:

1. Twelve-month Planner Pages- space for planning, tasks, budget, and notes

2. Expense Pages- for Winter, Spring, Summer, and Fall

3. Plant Log- record: plant name, type, plant details, fertilizer, soil amendments, pests, pest control, weeds, weed control, watering schedule, outcome (bloom and harvest), plant rating

4. Seed Inventory- variety, seed company, date purchased, quantity

5. Supplier List- company name, website, address, phone number, and products

6. Tool Inventory- tool list

7. Graph Paper- to sketch out garden plans

8. Wish List- collection page for jotting down wants and needs for the garden

JANUARY

PLANNING	TASKS

BUDGET	NOTES

FEBRUARY

PLANNING	TASKS

BUDGET	NOTES

MARCH

PLANNING	TASKS

BUDGET	NOTES

APRIL

PLANNING	TASKS

BUDGET	NOTES

MAY

PLANNING	TASKS

BUDGET	NOTES

JUNE

PLANNING	TASKS

BUDGET	NOTES

JULY

PLANNING	TASKS

BUDGET	NOTES

AUGUST

PLANNING	TASKS

BUDGET	NOTES

SEPTEMBER

PLANNING	TASKS

BUDGET	NOTES

OCTOBER

PLANNING	TASKS

BUDGET	NOTES

NOVEMBER

PLANNING	TASKS

BUDGET	NOTES

DECEMBER

PLANNING	TO DO LIST

BUDGET	NOTES

WINTER EXPENSES

ITEM	DESCRIPTION	QUANITY	PRICE

SPRING EXPENSES

ITEM	DESCRIPTION	QUANITY	PRICE

SUMMER EXPENSES

ITEM	DESCRIPTION	QUANITY	PRICE

FALL EXPENSES

ITEM	DESCRIPTION	QUANITY	PRICE

PLANT LOG

PLANT NAME	
SCIENTIFIC NAME	
SUPPLIER	COST

PLANT TYPE

☐ ANNUAL ☐ BIENNIAL ☐ BULB ☐ FLOWER ☐ FRUIT ☐ HERB

☐ PERENNIAL ☐ SEEDLING ☐ SHRUB ☐ SUCCULENT ☐ TRANSPLANT

☐ TREE ☐ VEGETABLE

PLANT DETAILS

DATE PLANTED	DATE GERMINATED	LOCATION	LIGHT CONDITIONS
			SUN ☐ PART SUN ☐ SHADE ☐

FERTILIZER	
SOIL AMENDMENTS	
PESTS	
PEST CONTROL	
WEEDS	
WEED CONTROL	

WATER

WATER SCHEDULE	RAINFALL
MON TUES WED THUR FRI SAT SUN	MON TUES WED THUR FRI SAT SUN

OUTCOME

BLOOM	HARVEST

PLANT RATING ✿ ✿ ✿ ✿ ✿

PLANT LOG

PLANT NAME	
SCIENTIFIC NAME	
SUPPLIER	COST

PLANT TYPE

- [ ] ANNUAL
- [ ] BIENNIAL
- [ ] BULB
- [ ] FLOWER
- [ ] FRUIT
- [ ] HERB
- [ ] PERENNIAL
- [ ] SEEDLING
- [ ] SHRUB
- [ ] SUCCULENT
- [ ] TRANSPLANT
- [ ] TREE
- [ ] VEGETABLE

PLANT DETAILS

DATE PLANTED	DATE GERMINATED	LOCATION	LIGHT CONDITIONS
			SUN [ ] PART SUN [ ] SHADE [ ]

FERTILIZER	
SOIL AMENDMENTS	
PESTS	
PEST CONTROL	
WEEDS	
WEED CONTROL	

WATER

WATER SCHEDULE	RAINFALL
MON TUES WED THUR FRI SAT SUN	MON TUES WED THUR FRI SAT SUN

OUTCOME

BLOOM	HARVEST

PLANT RATING ✿ ✿ ✿ ✿ ✿

PLANT LOG

PLANT NAME	
SCIENTIFIC NAME	

SUPPLIER		COST	

PLANT TYPE

- [ ] ANNUAL [ ] BIENNIAL [ ] BULB [ ] FLOWER [ ] FRUIT [ ] HERB
- [ ] PERENNIAL [ ] SEEDLING [ ] SHRUB [ ] SUCCULENT [ ] TRANSPLANT
- [ ] TREE [ ] VEGETABLE

PLANT DETAILS

DATE PLANTED	DATE GERMINATED	LOCATION	LIGHT CONDITIONS
			SUN [ ] PART SUN [ ] SHADE [ ]

FERTILIZER	
SOIL AMENDMENTS	
PESTS	
PEST CONTROL	
WEEDS	
WEED CONTROL	

WATER

WATER SCHEDULE	RAINFALL
MON TUES WED THUR FRI SAT SUN	MON TUES WED THUR FRI SAT SUN

OUTCOME

BLOOM	HARVEST

PLANT RATING

PLANT LOG

PLANT NAME	
SCIENTIFIC NAME	
SUPPLIER	COST

PLANT TYPE

- ☐ ANNUAL ☐ BIENNIAL ☐ BULB ☐ FLOWER ☐ FRUIT ☐ HERB
- ☐ PERENNIAL ☐ SEEDLING ☐ SHRUB ☐ SUCCULENT ☐ TRANSPLANT
- ☐ TREE ☐ VEGETABLE

PLANT DETAILS

DATE PLANTED	DATE GERMINATED	LOCATION	LIGHT CONDITIONS
			SUN ☐ PART SUN ☐ SHADE ☐

FERTILIZER	
SOIL AMENDMENTS	
PESTS	
PEST CONTROL	
WEEDS	
WEED CONTROL	

WATER

WATER SCHEDULE	RAINFALL
MON TUES WED THUR FRI SAT SUN	MON TUES WED THUR FRI SAT SUN

OUTCOME

BLOOM	HARVEST

PLANT RATING 🌿 🌿 🌿 🌿 🌿

PLANT LOG

PLANT NAME	
SCIENTIFIC NAME	
SUPPLIER	**COST**

PLANT TYPE

☐ ANNUAL ☐ BIENNIAL ☐ BULB ☐ FLOWER ☐ FRUIT ☐ HERB

☐ PERENNIAL ☐ SEEDLING ☐ SHRUB ☐ SUCCULENT ☐ TRANSPLANT

☐ TREE ☐ VEGETABLE

PLANT DETAILS

DATE PLANTED	DATE GERMINATED	LOCATION	LIGHT CONDITIONS
			SUN ☐ PART SUN ☐ SHADE ☐

FERTILIZER	
SOIL AMENDMENTS	
PESTS	
PEST CONTROL	
WEEDS	
WEED CONTROL	

WATER

WATER SCHEDULE	RAINFALL
MON TUES WED THUR FRI SAT SUN	MON TUES WED THUR FRI SAT SUN

OUTCOME

BLOOM	HARVEST

PLANT RATING 🍃🍃🍃🍃🍃

PLANT LOG

PLANT NAME	
SCIENTIFIC NAME	

SUPPLIER		COST	

PLANT TYPE

- ☐ ANNUAL ☐ BIENNIAL ☐ BULB ☐ FLOWER ☐ FRUIT ☐ HERB
- ☐ PERENNIAL ☐ SEEDLING ☐ SHRUB ☐ SUCCULENT ☐ TRANSPLANT
- ☐ TREE ☐ VEGETABLE

PLANT DETAILS

DATE PLANTED	DATE GERMINATED	LOCATION	LIGHT CONDITIONS
			SUN ☐ PART SUN ☐ SHADE ☐

FERTILIZER	
SOIL AMENDMENTS	
PESTS	
PEST CONTROL	
WEEDS	
WEED CONTROL	

WATER

WATER SCHEDULE	RAINFALL
MON TUES WED THUR FRI SAT SUN	MON TUES WED THUR FRI SAT SUN

OUTCOME

BLOOM	HARVEST

PLANT RATING 🍃 🍃 🍃 🍃 🍃

PLANT LOG

PLANT NAME	
SCIENTIFIC NAME	

SUPPLIER		COST

PLANT TYPE

☐ ANNUAL ☐ BIENNIAL ☐ BULB ☐ FLOWER ☐ FRUIT ☐ HERB
☐ PERENNIAL ☐ SEEDLING ☐ SHRUB ☐ SUCCULENT ☐ TRANSPLANT
☐ TREE ☐ VEGETABLE

PLANT DETAILS

DATE PLANTED	DATE GERMINATED	LOCATION	LIGHT CONDITIONS
			SUN ☐ PART SUN ☐ SHADE ☐

FERTILIZER	
SOIL AMENDMENTS	
PESTS	
PEST CONTROL	
WEEDS	
WEED CONTROL	

WATER

WATER SCHEDULE	RAINFALL
MON TUES WED THUR FRI SAT SUN	MON TUES WED THUR FRI SAT SUN

OUTCOME

BLOOM	HARVEST

PLANT RATING 🍃🍃🍃🍃🍃

PLANT LOG

PLANT NAME	
SCIENTIFIC NAME	

SUPPLIER		COST	

PLANT TYPE

☐ ANNUAL ☐ BIENNIAL ☐ BULB ☐ FLOWER ☐ FRUIT ☐ HERB
☐ PERENNIAL ☐ SEEDLING ☐ SHRUB ☐ SUCCULENT ☐ TRANSPLANT
☐ TREE ☐ VEGETABLE

PLANT DETAILS

DATE PLANTED	DATE GERMINATED	LOCATION	LIGHT CONDITIONS
			SUN ☐ PART SUN ☐ SHADE ☐

FERTILIZER	
SOIL AMENDMENTS	
PESTS	
PEST CONTROL	
WEEDS	
WEED CONTROL	

WATER

WATER SCHEDULE	RAINFALL
MON TUES WED THUR FRI SAT SUN	MON TUES WED THUR FRI SAT SUN

OUTCOME

BLOOM	HARVEST

PLANT RATING 🍃🍃🍃🍃🍃

PLANT LOG

PLANT NAME	
SCIENTIFIC NAME	

SUPPLIER		COST	

PLANT TYPE

☐ ANNUAL ☐ BIENNIAL ☐ BULB ☐ FLOWER ☐ FRUIT ☐ HERB

☐ PERENNIAL ☐ SEEDLING ☐ SHRUB ☐ SUCCULENT ☐ TRANSPLANT

☐ TREE ☐ VEGETABLE

PLANT DETAILS

DATE PLANTED	DATE GERMINATED	LOCATION	LIGHT CONDITIONS
			SUN ☐ PART SUN ☐ SHADE ☐

FERTILIZER	
SOIL AMENDMENTS	
PESTS	
PEST CONTROL	
WEEDS	
WEED CONTROL	

WATER

WATER SCHEDULE	RAINFALL
MON TUES WED THUR FRI SAT SUN	MON TUES WED THUR FRI SAT SUN

OUTCOME

BLOOM	HARVEST

PLANT RATING 🍃 🍃 🍃 🍃 🍃

PLANT LOG

PLANT NAME	
SCIENTIFIC NAME	
SUPPLIER	COST

PLANT TYPE

- [ ] ANNUAL [ ] BIENNIAL [ ] BULB [ ] FLOWER [ ] FRUIT [ ] HERB
- [ ] PERENNIAL [ ] SEEDLING [ ] SHRUB [ ] SUCCULENT [ ] TRANSPLANT
- [ ] TREE [ ] VEGETABLE

PLANT DETAILS

DATE PLANTED	DATE GERMINATED	LOCATION	LIGHT CONDITIONS
			SUN [ ] PART SUN [ ] SHADE [ ]

FERTILIZER	
SOIL AMENDMENTS	
PESTS	
PEST CONTROL	
WEEDS	
WEED CONTROL	

WATER

WATER SCHEDULE	RAINFALL
MON TUES WED THUR FRI SAT SUN	MON TUES WED THUR FRI SAT SUN

OUTCOME

BLOOM	HARVEST

PLANT RATING 🌿 🌿 🌿 🌿 🌿

PLANT LOG

PLANT NAME	
SCIENTIFIC NAME	
SUPPLIER	COST

PLANT TYPE

☐ ANNUAL ☐ BIENNIAL ☐ BULB ☐ FLOWER ☐ FRUIT ☐ HERB

☐ PERENNIAL ☐ SEEDLING ☐ SHRUB ☐ SUCCULENT ☐ TRANSPLANT

☐ TREE ☐ VEGETABLE

PLANT DETAILS

DATE PLANTED	DATE GERMINATED	LOCATION	LIGHT CONDITIONS
			SUN ☐ PART SUN ☐ SHADE ☐

FERTILIZER	
SOIL AMENDMENTS	
PESTS	
PEST CONTROL	
WEEDS	
WEED CONTROL	

WATER

WATER SCHEDULE	RAINFALL
MON TUES WED THUR FRI SAT SUN	MON TUES WED THUR FRI SAT SUN

OUTCOME

BLOOM	HARVEST

PLANT RATING ✿ ✿ ✿ ✿ ✿

PLANT LOG

PLANT NAME	
SCIENTIFIC NAME	
SUPPLIER	COST

PLANT TYPE

☐ ANNUAL ☐ BIENNIAL ☐ BULB ☐ FLOWER ☐ FRUIT ☐ HERB
☐ PERENNIAL ☐ SEEDLING ☐ SHRUB ☐ SUCCULENT ☐ TRANSPLANT
☐ TREE ☐ VEGETABLE

PLANT DETAILS

DATE PLANTED	DATE GERMINATED	LOCATION	LIGHT CONDITIONS
			SUN ☐ PART SUN ☐ SHADE ☐

FERTILIZER	
SOIL AMENDMENTS	
PESTS	
PEST CONTROL	
WEEDS	
WEED CONTROL	

WATER

WATER SCHEDULE	RAINFALL
MON TUES WED THUR FRI SAT SUN	MON TUES WED THUR FRI SAT SUN

OUTCOME

BLOOM	HARVEST

PLANT RATING 🍃🍃🍃🍃🍃

PLANT LOG

PLANT NAME	
SCIENTIFIC NAME	

SUPPLIER		COST	

PLANT TYPE

- [ ] ANNUAL [ ] BIENNIAL [ ] BULB [ ] FLOWER [ ] FRUIT [ ] HERB
- [ ] PERENNIAL [ ] SEEDLING [ ] SHRUB [ ] SUCCULENT [ ] TRANSPLANT
- [ ] TREE [ ] VEGETABLE

PLANT DETAILS

DATE PLANTED	DATE GERMINATED	LOCATION	LIGHT CONDITIONS
			SUN [ ] PART SUN [ ] SHADE [ ]

FERTILIZER	
SOIL AMENDMENTS	
PESTS	
PEST CONTROL	
WEEDS	
WEED CONTROL	

WATER

WATER SCHEDULE	RAINFALL
MON TUES WED THUR FRI SAT SUN	MON TUES WED THUR FRI SAT SUN

OUTCOME

BLOOM	HARVEST

PLANT RATING 🍃🍃🍃🍃🍃

PLANT LOG

PLANT NAME	
SCIENTIFIC NAME	
SUPPLIER	COST

PLANT TYPE

- [ ] ANNUAL
- [ ] BIENNIAL
- [ ] BULB
- [ ] FLOWER
- [ ] FRUIT
- [ ] HERB
- [ ] PERENNIAL
- [ ] SEEDLING
- [ ] SHRUB
- [ ] SUCCULENT
- [ ] TRANSPLANT
- [ ] TREE
- [ ] VEGETABLE

PLANT DETAILS

DATE PLANTED	DATE GERMINATED	LOCATION	LIGHT CONDITIONS
			SUN ☐ PART SUN ☐ SHADE ☐

FERTILIZER	
SOIL AMENDMENTS	
PESTS	
PEST CONTROL	
WEEDS	
WEED CONTROL	

WATER

WATER SCHEDULE	RAINFALL
MON TUES WED THUR FRI SAT SUN	MON TUES WED THUR FRI SAT SUN

OUTCOME

BLOOM	HARVEST

PLANT RATING 🌿 🌿 🌿 🌿 🌿

PLANT LOG

PLANT NAME	
SCIENTIFIC NAME	
SUPPLIER	COST

PLANT TYPE

- [ ] ANNUAL
- [ ] BIENNIAL
- [ ] BULB
- [ ] FLOWER
- [ ] FRUIT
- [ ] HERB
- [ ] PERENNIAL
- [ ] SEEDLING
- [ ] SHRUB
- [ ] SUCCULENT
- [ ] TRANSPLANT
- [ ] TREE
- [ ] VEGETABLE

PLANT DETAILS

DATE PLANTED	DATE GERMINATED	LOCATION	LIGHT CONDITIONS
			SUN [ ] PART SUN [ ] SHADE [ ]

FERTILIZER	
SOIL AMENDMENTS	
PESTS	
PEST CONTROL	
WEEDS	
WEED CONTROL	

WATER

WATER SCHEDULE	RAINFALL
MON TUES WED THUR FRI SAT SUN	MON TUES WED THUR FRI SAT SUN

OUTCOME

BLOOM	HARVEST

PLANT RATING 🍃 🍃 🍃 🍃 🍃

PLANT LOG

PLANT NAME	
SCIENTIFIC NAME	

SUPPLIER		COST	

PLANT TYPE

- ☐ ANNUAL
- ☐ BIENNIAL
- ☐ BULB
- ☐ FLOWER
- ☐ FRUIT
- ☐ HERB
- ☐ PERENNIAL
- ☐ SEEDLING
- ☐ SHRUB
- ☐ SUCCULENT
- ☐ TRANSPLANT
- ☐ TREE
- ☐ VEGETABLE

PLANT DETAILS

DATE PLANTED	DATE GERMINATED	LOCATION	LIGHT CONDITIONS
			SUN ☐ PART SUN ☐ SHADE ☐

FERTILIZER	
SOIL AMENDMENTS	
PESTS	
PEST CONTROL	
WEEDS	
WEED CONTROL	

WATER

WATER SCHEDULE	RAINFALL
MON TUES WED THUR FRI SAT SUN	MON TUES WED THUR FRI SAT SUN

OUTCOME

BLOOM	HARVEST

PLANT RATING 🍃🍃🍃🍃🍃

PLANT LOG

PLANT NAME	
SCIENTIFIC NAME	

SUPPLIER		COST	

PLANT TYPE

☐ ANNUAL ☐ BIENNIAL ☐ BULB ☐ FLOWER ☐ FRUIT ☐ HERB

☐ PERENNIAL ☐ SEEDLING ☐ SHRUB ☐ SUCCULENT ☐ TRANSPLANT

☐ TREE ☐ VEGETABLE

PLANT DETAILS

DATE PLANTED	DATE GERMINATED	LOCATION	LIGHT CONDITIONS
			SUN ☐ PART SUN ☐ SHADE ☐

FERTILIZER	
SOIL AMENDMENTS	
PESTS	
PEST CONTROL	
WEEDS	
WEED CONTROL	

WATER

WATER SCHEDULE	RAINFALL
MON TUES WED THUR FRI SAT SUN	MON TUES WED THUR FRI SAT SUN

OUTCOME

BLOOM	HARVEST

PLANT RATING 🍃 🍃 🍃 🍃 🍃

PLANT LOG

PLANT NAME		
SCIENTIFIC NAME		
SUPPLIER		COST

PLANT TYPE

- [ ] ANNUAL [ ] BIENNIAL [ ] BULB [ ] FLOWER [ ] FRUIT [ ] HERB
- [ ] PERENNIAL [ ] SEEDLING [ ] SHRUB [ ] SUCCULENT [ ] TRANSPLANT
- [ ] TREE [ ] VEGETABLE

PLANT DETAILS

DATE PLANTED	DATE GERMINATED	LOCATION	LIGHT CONDITIONS
			SUN [ ] PART SUN [ ] SHADE [ ]

FERTILIZER	
SOIL AMENDMENTS	
PESTS	
PEST CONTROL	
WEEDS	
WEED CONTROL	

WATER

WATER SCHEDULE	RAINFALL
MON TUES WED THUR FRI SAT SUN	MON TUES WED THUR FRI SAT SUN

OUTCOME

BLOOM	HARVEST

PLANT RATING 🍃🍃🍃🍃🍃

PLANT LOG

PLANT NAME	
SCIENTIFIC NAME	
SUPPLIER	COST

PLANT TYPE

- [ ] ANNUAL [ ] BIENNIAL [ ] BULB [ ] FLOWER [ ] FRUIT [ ] HERB
- [ ] PERENNIAL [ ] SEEDLING [ ] SHRUB [ ] SUCCULENT [ ] TRANSPLANT
- [ ] TREE [ ] VEGETABLE

PLANT DETAILS

DATE PLANTED	DATE GERMINATED	LOCATION	LIGHT CONDITIONS
			SUN [ ] PART SUN [ ] SHADE [ ]

FERTILIZER	
SOIL AMENDMENTS	
PESTS	
PEST CONTROL	
WEEDS	
WEED CONTROL	

WATER

WATER SCHEDULE	RAINFALL
MON TUES WED THUR FRI SAT SUN	MON TUES WED THUR FRI SAT SUN

OUTCOME

BLOOM	HARVEST

PLANT RATING 🌿🌿🌿🌿🌿

PLANT LOG

PLANT NAME	
SCIENTIFIC NAME	

SUPPLIER		COST	

PLANT TYPE

☐ ANNUAL ☐ BIENNIAL ☐ BULB ☐ FLOWER ☐ FRUIT ☐ HERB
☐ PERENNIAL ☐ SEEDLING ☐ SHRUB ☐ SUCCULENT ☐ TRANSPLANT
☐ TREE ☐ VEGETABLE

PLANT DETAILS

DATE PLANTED	DATE GERMINATED	LOCATION	LIGHT CONDITIONS
			SUN ☐ PART SUN ☐ SHADE ☐

FERTILIZER	
SOIL AMENDMENTS	
PESTS	
PEST CONTROL	
WEEDS	
WEED CONTROL	

WATER

WATER SCHEDULE	RAINFALL
MON TUES WED THUR FRI SAT SUN	MON TUES WED THUR FRI SAT SUN

OUTCOME

BLOOM	HARVEST

PLANT RATING 🌿 🌿 🌿 🌿 🌿

PLANT LOG

PLANT NAME	
SCIENTIFIC NAME	

SUPPLIER		COST	

PLANT TYPE

- [ ] ANNUAL [ ] BIENNIAL [ ] BULB [ ] FLOWER [ ] FRUIT [ ] HERB
- [ ] PERENNIAL [ ] SEEDLING [ ] SHRUB [ ] SUCCULENT [ ] TRANSPLANT
- [ ] TREE [ ] VEGETABLE

PLANT DETAILS

DATE PLANTED	DATE GERMINATED	LOCATION	LIGHT CONDITIONS
			SUN [ ] PART SUN [ ] SHADE [ ]

FERTILIZER	
SOIL AMENDMENTS	
PESTS	
PEST CONTROL	
WEEDS	
WEED CONTROL	

WATER

WATER SCHEDULE	RAINFALL
MON TUES WED THUR FRI SAT SUN	MON TUES WED THUR FRI SAT SUN

OUTCOME

BLOOM	HARVEST

PLANT RATING 🍃🍃🍃🍃🍃

PLANT LOG

PLANT NAME	
SCIENTIFIC NAME	
SUPPLIER	COST

PLANT TYPE

- ☐ ANNUAL ☐ BIENNIAL ☐ BULB ☐ FLOWER ☐ FRUIT ☐ HERB
- ☐ PERENNIAL ☐ SEEDLING ☐ SHRUB ☐ SUCCULENT ☐ TRANSPLANT
- ☐ TREE ☐ VEGETABLE

PLANT DETAILS

DATE PLANTED	DATE GERMINATED	LOCATION	LIGHT CONDITIONS
			SUN ☐ PART SUN ☐ SHADE ☐

FERTILIZER	
SOIL AMENDMENTS	
PESTS	
PEST CONTROL	
WEEDS	
WEED CONTROL	

WATER

WATER SCHEDULE	RAINFALL
MON TUES WED THUR FRI SAT SUN	MON TUES WED THUR FRI SAT SUN

OUTCOME

BLOOM	HARVEST

PLANT RATING 🌿🌿🌿🌿🌿

PLANT LOG

PLANT NAME		
SCIENTIFIC NAME		
SUPPLIER		COST

PLANT TYPE

☐ ANNUAL ☐ BIENNIAL ☐ BULB ☐ FLOWER ☐ FRUIT ☐ HERB

☐ PERENNIAL ☐ SEEDLING ☐ SHRUB ☐ SUCCULENT ☐ TRANSPLANT

☐ TREE ☐ VEGETABLE

PLANT DETAILS

DATE PLANTED	DATE GERMINATED	LOCATION	LIGHT CONDITIONS
			SUN ☐ PART SUN ☐ SHADE ☐

FERTILIZER	
SOIL AMENDMENTS	
PESTS	
PEST CONTROL	
WEEDS	
WEED CONTROL	

WATER

WATER SCHEDULE	RAINFALL
MON TUES WED THUR FRI SAT SUN	MON TUES WED THUR FRI SAT SUN

OUTCOME

BLOOM	HARVEST

PLANT RATING 🍃 🍃 🍃 🍃 🍃

PLANT LOG

PLANT NAME	
SCIENTIFIC NAME	
SUPPLIER	COST

PLANT TYPE

- [ ] ANNUAL [ ] BIENNIAL [ ] BULB [ ] FLOWER [ ] FRUIT [ ] HERB
- [ ] PERENNIAL [ ] SEEDLING [ ] SHRUB [ ] SUCCULENT [ ] TRANSPLANT
- [ ] TREE [ ] VEGETABLE

PLANT DETAILS

DATE PLANTED	DATE GERMINATED	LOCATION	LIGHT CONDITIONS
			SUN [ ] PART SUN [ ] SHADE [ ]

FERTILIZER	
SOIL AMENDMENTS	
PESTS	
PEST CONTROL	
WEEDS	
WEED CONTROL	

WATER

WATER SCHEDULE	RAINFALL
MON TUES WED THUR FRI SAT SUN	MON TUES WED THUR FRI SAT SUN

OUTCOME

BLOOM	HARVEST

PLANT RATING

PLANT LOG

PLANT NAME	
SCIENTIFIC NAME	
SUPPLIER	COST

PLANT TYPE

- [ ] ANNUAL [ ] BIENNIAL [ ] BULB [ ] FLOWER [ ] FRUIT [ ] HERB
- [ ] PERENNIAL [ ] SEEDLING [ ] SHRUB [ ] SUCCULENT [ ] TRANSPLANT
- [ ] TREE [ ] VEGETABLE

PLANT DETAILS

DATE PLANTED	DATE GERMINATED	LOCATION	LIGHT CONDITIONS
			SUN [ ] PART SUN [ ] SHADE [ ]

FERTILIZER	
SOIL AMENDMENTS	
PESTS	
PEST CONTROL	
WEEDS	
WEED CONTROL	

WATER

WATER SCHEDULE	RAINFALL
MON TUES WED THUR FRI SAT SUN	MON TUES WED THUR FRI SAT SUN

OUTCOME

BLOOM	HARVEST

PLANT RATING

PLANT LOG

PLANT NAME	
SCIENTIFIC NAME	

SUPPLIER		COST	

PLANT TYPE

- [ ] ANNUAL
- [ ] BIENNIAL
- [ ] BULB
- [ ] FLOWER
- [ ] FRUIT
- [ ] HERB
- [ ] PERENNIAL
- [ ] SEEDLING
- [ ] SHRUB
- [ ] SUCCULENT
- [ ] TRANSPLANT
- [ ] TREE
- [ ] VEGETABLE

PLANT DETAILS

DATE PLANTED	DATE GERMINATED	LOCATION	LIGHT CONDITIONS
			SUN [ ] PART SUN [ ] SHADE [ ]

FERTILIZER	
SOIL AMENDMENTS	
PESTS	
PEST CONTROL	
WEEDS	
WEED CONTROL	

WATER

WATER SCHEDULE	RAINFALL
MON TUES WED THUR FRI SAT SUN	MON TUES WED THUR FRI SAT SUN

OUTCOME

BLOOM	HARVEST

PLANT RATING 🍃🍃🍃🍃🍃

PLANT LOG

PLANT NAME	
SCIENTIFIC NAME	
SUPPLIER	COST

PLANT TYPE

☐ ANNUAL　☐ BIENNIAL　☐ BULB　☐ FLOWER　☐ FRUIT　☐ HERB
☐ PERENNIAL　☐ SEEDLING　☐ SHRUB　☐ SUCCULENT　☐ TRANSPLANT
☐ TREE　☐ VEGETABLE

PLANT DETAILS

DATE PLANTED	DATE GERMINATED	LOCATION	LIGHT CONDITIONS
			SUN ☐ PART SUN ☐ SHADE ☐

FERTILIZER	
SOIL AMENDMENTS	
PESTS	
PEST CONTROL	
WEEDS	
WEED CONTROL	

WATER

WATER SCHEDULE	RAINFALL
MON　TUES　WED　THUR　FRI　SAT　SUN	MON　TUES　WED　THUR　FRI　SAT　SUN

OUTCOME

BLOOM	HARVEST

PLANT RATING 🍃🍃🍃🍃🍃

PLANT LOG

PLANT NAME	
SCIENTIFIC NAME	

SUPPLIER		COST	

PLANT TYPE

- [ ] ANNUAL [ ] BIENNIAL [ ] BULB [ ] FLOWER [ ] FRUIT [ ] HERB
- [ ] PERENNIAL [ ] SEEDLING [ ] SHRUB [ ] SUCCULENT [ ] TRANSPLANT
- [ ] TREE [ ] VEGETABLE

PLANT DETAILS

DATE PLANTED	DATE GERMINATED	LOCATION	LIGHT CONDITIONS
			SUN [ ] PART SUN [ ] SHADE [ ]

FERTILIZER	
SOIL AMENDMENTS	
PESTS	
PEST CONTROL	
WEEDS	
WEED CONTROL	

WATER

WATER SCHEDULE	RAINFALL
MON TUES WED THUR FRI SAT SUN	MON TUES WED THUR FRI SAT SUN

OUTCOME

BLOOM	HARVEST

PLANT RATING 🍃 🍃 🍃 🍃 🍃

PLANT LOG

PLANT NAME		
SCIENTIFIC NAME		
SUPPLIER		COST

PLANT TYPE

☐ ANNUAL ☐ BIENNIAL ☐ BULB ☐ FLOWER ☐ FRUIT ☐ HERB
☐ PERENNIAL ☐ SEEDLING ☐ SHRUB ☐ SUCCULENT ☐ TRANSPLANT
☐ TREE ☐ VEGETABLE

PLANT DETAILS

DATE PLANTED	DATE GERMINATED	LOCATION	LIGHT CONDITIONS
			SUN ☐ PART SUN ☐ SHADE ☐

FERTILIZER	
SOIL AMENDMENTS	
PESTS	
PEST CONTROL	
WEEDS	
WEED CONTROL	

WATER

WATER SCHEDULE	RAINFALL
MON TUES WED THUR FRI SAT SUN	MON TUES WED THUR FRI SAT SUN

OUTCOME

BLOOM	HARVEST

PLANT RATING

PLANT LOG

PLANT NAME	
SCIENTIFIC NAME	

SUPPLIER		COST	

PLANT TYPE

- [ ] ANNUAL [ ] BIENNIAL [ ] BULB [ ] FLOWER [ ] FRUIT [ ] HERB
- [ ] PERENNIAL [ ] SEEDLING [ ] SHRUB [ ] SUCCULENT [ ] TRANSPLANT
- [ ] TREE [ ] VEGETABLE

PLANT DETAILS

DATE PLANTED	DATE GERMINATED	LOCATION	LIGHT CONDITIONS
			SUN [ ] PART SUN [ ] SHADE [ ]

FERTILIZER	
SOIL AMENDMENTS	
PESTS	
PEST CONTROL	
WEEDS	
WEED CONTROL	

WATER

WATER SCHEDULE	RAINFALL
MON TUES WED THUR FRI SAT SUN	MON TUES WED THUR FRI SAT SUN

OUTCOME

BLOOM	HARVEST

PLANT RATING 🌿 🌿 🌿 🌿 🌿

PLANT LOG

PLANT NAME	
SCIENTIFIC NAME	

SUPPLIER		COST	

PLANT TYPE

- [ ] ANNUAL [ ] BIENNIAL [ ] BULB [ ] FLOWER [ ] FRUIT [ ] HERB
- [ ] PERENNIAL [ ] SEEDLING [ ] SHRUB [ ] SUCCULENT [ ] TRANSPLANT
- [ ] TREE [ ] VEGETABLE

PLANT DETAILS

DATE PLANTED	DATE GERMINATED	LOCATION	LIGHT CONDITIONS
			SUN [ ] PART SUN [ ] SHADE [ ]

FERTILIZER	
SOIL AMENDMENTS	
PESTS	
PEST CONTROL	
WEEDS	
WEED CONTROL	

WATER

WATER SCHEDULE	RAINFALL
MON TUES WED THUR FRI SAT SUN	MON TUES WED THUR FRI SAT SUN

OUTCOME

BLOOM	HARVEST

PLANT RATING 🍃 🍃 🍃 🍃 🍃

PLANT LOG

PLANT NAME	
SCIENTIFIC NAME	

SUPPLIER		COST	

PLANT TYPE

☐ ANNUAL ☐ BIENNIAL ☐ BULB ☐ FLOWER ☐ FRUIT ☐ HERB
☐ PERENNIAL ☐ SEEDLING ☐ SHRUB ☐ SUCCULENT ☐ TRANSPLANT
☐ TREE ☐ VEGETABLE

PLANT DETAILS

DATE PLANTED	DATE GERMINATED	LOCATION	LIGHT CONDITIONS
			SUN ☐ PART SUN ☐ SHADE ☐

FERTILIZER	
SOIL AMENDMENTS	
PESTS	
PEST CONTROL	
WEEDS	
WEED CONTROL	

WATER

WATER SCHEDULE	RAINFALL
MON TUES WED THUR FRI SAT SUN	MON TUES WED THUR FRI SAT SUN

OUTCOME

BLOOM	HARVEST

PLANT RATING 🍃 🍃 🍃 🍃 🍃

PLANT LOG

PLANT NAME	
SCIENTIFIC NAME	
SUPPLIER	COST

PLANT TYPE

- [ ] ANNUAL
- [ ] BIENNIAL
- [ ] BULB
- [ ] FLOWER
- [ ] FRUIT
- [ ] HERB
- [ ] PERENNIAL
- [ ] SEEDLING
- [ ] SHRUB
- [ ] SUCCULENT
- [ ] TRANSPLANT
- [ ] TREE
- [ ] VEGETABLE

PLANT DETAILS

DATE PLANTED	DATE GERMINATED	LOCATION	LIGHT CONDITIONS
			SUN [ ] PART SUN [ ] SHADE [ ]

FERTILIZER	
SOIL AMENDMENTS	
PESTS	
PEST CONTROL	
WEEDS	
WEED CONTROL	

WATER

WATER SCHEDULE	RAINFALL
MON TUES WED THUR FRI SAT SUN	MON TUES WED THUR FRI SAT SUN

OUTCOME

BLOOM	HARVEST

PLANT RATING 🍃🍃🍃🍃🍃

PLANT LOG

PLANT NAME		
SCIENTIFIC NAME		
SUPPLIER		COST

PLANT TYPE

☐ ANNUAL ☐ BIENNIAL ☐ BULB ☐ FLOWER ☐ FRUIT ☐ HERB

☐ PERENNIAL ☐ SEEDLING ☐ SHRUB ☐ SUCCULENT ☐ TRANSPLANT

☐ TREE ☐ VEGETABLE

PLANT DETAILS

DATE PLANTED	DATE GERMINATED	LOCATION	LIGHT CONDITIONS
			SUN ☐ PART SUN ☐ SHADE ☐

FERTILIZER	
SOIL AMENDMENTS	
PESTS	
PEST CONTROL	
WEEDS	
WEED CONTROL	

WATER

WATER SCHEDULE	RAINFALL
MON TUES WED THUR FRI SAT SUN	MON TUES WED THUR FRI SAT SUN

OUTCOME

BLOOM	HARVEST

PLANT RATING 🍃 🍃 🍃 🍃 🍃

PLANT LOG

PLANT NAME	
SCIENTIFIC NAME	
SUPPLIER	COST

PLANT TYPE

☐ ANNUAL ☐ BIENNIAL ☐ BULB ☐ FLOWER ☐ FRUIT ☐ HERB
☐ PERENNIAL ☐ SEEDLING ☐ SHRUB ☐ SUCCULENT ☐ TRANSPLANT
☐ TREE ☐ VEGETABLE

PLANT DETAILS

DATE PLANTED	DATE GERMINATED	LOCATION	LIGHT CONDITIONS
			SUN ☐ PART SUN ☐ SHADE ☐

FERTILIZER	
SOIL AMENDMENTS	
PESTS	
PEST CONTROL	
WEEDS	
WEED CONTROL	

WATER

WATER SCHEDULE	RAINFALL
MON TUES WED THUR FRI SAT SUN	MON TUES WED THUR FRI SAT SUN

OUTCOME

BLOOM	HARVEST

PLANT RATING 🍃 🍃 🍃 🍃 🍃

PLANT LOG

PLANT NAME	
SCIENTIFIC NAME	

SUPPLIER		COST	

PLANT TYPE

- [ ] ANNUAL
- [ ] BIENNIAL
- [ ] BULB
- [ ] FLOWER
- [ ] FRUIT
- [ ] HERB
- [ ] PERENNIAL
- [ ] SEEDLING
- [ ] SHRUB
- [ ] SUCCULENT
- [ ] TRANSPLANT
- [ ] TREE
- [ ] VEGETABLE

PLANT DETAILS

DATE PLANTED	DATE GERMINATED	LOCATION	LIGHT CONDITIONS
			SUN [ ] PART SUN [ ] SHADE [ ]

FERTILIZER	
SOIL AMENDMENTS	
PESTS	
PEST CONTROL	
WEEDS	
WEED CONTROL	

WATER

WATER SCHEDULE	RAINFALL
MON TUES WED THUR FRI SAT SUN	MON TUES WED THUR FRI SAT SUN

OUTCOME

BLOOM	HARVEST

PLANT RATING 🍃🍃🍃🍃🍃

PLANT LOG

PLANT NAME	
SCIENTIFIC NAME	

SUPPLIER		COST	

PLANT TYPE

☐ ANNUAL ☐ BIENNIAL ☐ BULB ☐ FLOWER ☐ FRUIT ☐ HERB
☐ PERENNIAL ☐ SEEDLING ☐ SHRUB ☐ SUCCULENT ☐ TRANSPLANT
☐ TREE ☐ VEGETABLE

PLANT DETAILS

DATE PLANTED	DATE GERMINATED	LOCATION	LIGHT CONDITIONS
			SUN ☐ PART SUN ☐ SHADE ☐

FERTILIZER	
SOIL AMENDMENTS	
PESTS	
PEST CONTROL	
WEEDS	
WEED CONTROL	

WATER

WATER SCHEDULE	RAINFALL
MON TUES WED THUR FRI SAT SUN	MON TUES WED THUR FRI SAT SUN

OUTCOME

BLOOM	HARVEST

PLANT RATING 🌿🌿🌿🌿🌿

PLANT LOG

PLANT NAME	
SCIENTIFIC NAME	
SUPPLIER	COST

PLANT TYPE

- [ ] ANNUAL
- [ ] BIENNIAL
- [ ] BULB
- [ ] FLOWER
- [ ] FRUIT
- [ ] HERB
- [ ] PERENNIAL
- [ ] SEEDLING
- [ ] SHRUB
- [ ] SUCCULENT
- [ ] TRANSPLANT
- [ ] TREE
- [ ] VEGETABLE

PLANT DETAILS

DATE PLANTED	DATE GERMINATED	LOCATION	LIGHT CONDITIONS
			SUN [ ] PART SUN [ ] SHADE [ ]

FERTILIZER	
SOIL AMENDMENTS	
PESTS	
PEST CONTROL	
WEEDS	
WEED CONTROL	

WATER

WATER SCHEDULE	RAINFALL
MON TUES WED THUR FRI SAT SUN	MON TUES WED THUR FRI SAT SUN

OUTCOME

BLOOM	HARVEST

PLANT RATING 🍃🍃🍃🍃🍃

PLANT LOG

PLANT NAME	
SCIENTIFIC NAME	

SUPPLIER		COST

PLANT TYPE

☐ ANNUAL ☐ BIENNIAL ☐ BULB ☐ FLOWER ☐ FRUIT ☐ HERB
☐ PERENNIAL ☐ SEEDLING ☐ SHRUB ☐ SUCCULENT ☐ TRANSPLANT
☐ TREE ☐ VEGETABLE

PLANT DETAILS

DATE PLANTED	DATE GERMINATED	LOCATION	LIGHT CONDITIONS
			SUN ☐ PART SUN ☐ SHADE ☐

FERTILIZER	
SOIL AMENDMENTS	
PESTS	
PEST CONTROL	
WEEDS	
WEED CONTROL	

WATER

WATER SCHEDULE	RAINFALL
MON TUES WED THUR FRI SAT SUN	MON TUES WED THUR FRI SAT SUN

OUTCOME

BLOOM	HARVEST

PLANT RATING 🍃🍃🍃🍃🍃

PLANT LOG

PLANT NAME	
SCIENTIFIC NAME	
SUPPLIER	COST

PLANT TYPE

- [ ] ANNUAL
- [ ] BIENNIAL
- [ ] BULB
- [ ] FLOWER
- [ ] FRUIT
- [ ] HERB
- [ ] PERENNIAL
- [ ] SEEDLING
- [ ] SHRUB
- [ ] SUCCULENT
- [ ] TRANSPLANT
- [ ] TREE
- [ ] VEGETABLE

PLANT DETAILS

DATE PLANTED	DATE GERMINATED	LOCATION	LIGHT CONDITIONS
			SUN [ ] PART SUN [ ] SHADE [ ]

FERTILIZER	
SOIL AMENDMENTS	
PESTS	
PEST CONTROL	
WEEDS	
WEED CONTROL	

WATER

WATER SCHEDULE	RAINFALL
MON TUES WED THUR FRI SAT SUN	MON TUES WED THUR FRI SAT SUN

OUTCOME

BLOOM	HARVEST

PLANT RATING 🍃🍃🍃🍃🍃

PLANT LOG

PLANT NAME	
SCIENTIFIC NAME	

SUPPLIER		COST	

PLANT TYPE

- ☐ ANNUAL ☐ BIENNIAL ☐ BULB ☐ FLOWER ☐ FRUIT ☐ HERB
- ☐ PERENNIAL ☐ SEEDLING ☐ SHRUB ☐ SUCCULENT ☐ TRANSPLANT
- ☐ TREE ☐ VEGETABLE

PLANT DETAILS

DATE PLANTED	DATE GERMINATED	LOCATION	LIGHT CONDITIONS
			SUN ☐ PART SUN ☐ SHADE ☐

FERTILIZER	
SOIL AMENDMENTS	
PESTS	
PEST CONTROL	
WEEDS	
WEED CONTROL	

WATER

WATER SCHEDULE	RAINFALL
MON TUES WED THUR FRI SAT SUN	MON TUES WED THUR FRI SAT SUN

OUTCOME

BLOOM	HARVEST

PLANT RATING ⬦ ⬦ ⬦ ⬦ ⬦

PLANT LOG

PLANT NAME	
SCIENTIFIC NAME	
SUPPLIER	COST

PLANT TYPE

- [ ] ANNUAL [ ] BIENNIAL [ ] BULB [ ] FLOWER [ ] FRUIT [ ] HERB
- [ ] PERENNIAL [ ] SEEDLING [ ] SHRUB [ ] SUCCULENT [ ] TRANSPLANT
- [ ] TREE [ ] VEGETABLE

PLANT DETAILS

DATE PLANTED	DATE GERMINATED	LOCATION	LIGHT CONDITIONS
			SUN [ ] PART SUN [ ] SHADE [ ]

FERTILIZER	
SOIL AMENDMENTS	
PESTS	
PEST CONTROL	
WEEDS	
WEED CONTROL	

WATER

WATER SCHEDULE	RAINFALL
MON TUES WED THUR FRI SAT SUN	MON TUES WED THUR FRI SAT SUN

OUTCOME

BLOOM	HARVEST

PLANT RATING 🍃 🍃 🍃 🍃 🍃

PLANT LOG

PLANT NAME	
SCIENTIFIC NAME	
SUPPLIER	COST

PLANT TYPE

☐ ANNUAL ☐ BIENNIAL ☐ BULB ☐ FLOWER ☐ FRUIT ☐ HERB
☐ PERENNIAL ☐ SEEDLING ☐ SHRUB ☐ SUCCULENT ☐ TRANSPLANT
☐ TREE ☐ VEGETABLE

PLANT DETAILS

DATE PLANTED	DATE GERMINATED	LOCATION	LIGHT CONDITIONS
			SUN ☐ PART SUN ☐ SHADE ☐

FERTILIZER	
SOIL AMENDMENTS	
PESTS	
PEST CONTROL	
WEEDS	
WEED CONTROL	

WATER

WATER SCHEDULE	RAINFALL
MON TUES WED THUR FRI SAT SUN	MON TUES WED THUR FRI SAT SUN

OUTCOME

BLOOM	HARVEST

PLANT RATING 🌿🌿🌿🌿🌿

PLANT LOG

PLANT NAME	
SCIENTIFIC NAME	

SUPPLIER		COST	

PLANT TYPE

- ☐ ANNUAL
- ☐ BIENNIAL
- ☐ BULB
- ☐ FLOWER
- ☐ FRUIT
- ☐ HERB
- ☐ PERENNIAL
- ☐ SEEDLING
- ☐ SHRUB
- ☐ SUCCULENT
- ☐ TRANSPLANT
- ☐ TREE
- ☐ VEGETABLE

PLANT DETAILS

DATE PLANTED	DATE GERMINATED	LOCATION	LIGHT CONDITIONS
			SUN ☐ PART SUN ☐ SHADE ☐

FERTILIZER	
SOIL AMENDMENTS	
PESTS	
PEST CONTROL	
WEEDS	
WEED CONTROL	

WATER

WATER SCHEDULE	RAINFALL
MON TUES WED THUR FRI SAT SUN	MON TUES WED THUR FRI SAT SUN

OUTCOME

BLOOM	HARVEST

PLANT RATING 🍃🍃🍃🍃🍃

PLANT LOG

PLANT NAME	
SCIENTIFIC NAME	
SUPPLIER	COST

PLANT TYPE

☐ ANNUAL ☐ BIENNIAL ☐ BULB ☐ FLOWER ☐ FRUIT ☐ HERB

☐ PERENNIAL ☐ SEEDLING ☐ SHRUB ☐ SUCCULENT ☐ TRANSPLANT

☐ TREE ☐ VEGETABLE

PLANT DETAILS

DATE PLANTED	DATE GERMINATED	LOCATION	LIGHT CONDITIONS
			SUN ☐ PART SUN ☐ SHADE ☐

FERTILIZER	
SOIL AMENDMENTS	
PESTS	
PEST CONTROL	
WEEDS	
WEED CONTROL	

WATER

WATER SCHEDULE	RAINFALL
MON TUES WED THUR FRI SAT SUN	MON TUES WED THUR FRI SAT SUN

OUTCOME

BLOOM	HARVEST

PLANT RATING 🌿🌿🌿🌿🌿

PLANT LOG

PLANT NAME	
SCIENTIFIC NAME	
SUPPLIER	COST

PLANT TYPE

- ☐ ANNUAL ☐ BIENNIAL ☐ BULB ☐ FLOWER ☐ FRUIT ☐ HERB
- ☐ PERENNIAL ☐ SEEDLING ☐ SHRUB ☐ SUCCULENT ☐ TRANSPLANT
- ☐ TREE ☐ VEGETABLE

PLANT DETAILS

DATE PLANTED	DATE GERMINATED	LOCATION	LIGHT CONDITIONS
			SUN ☐ PART SUN ☐ SHADE ☐

FERTILIZER	
SOIL AMENDMENTS	
PESTS	
PEST CONTROL	
WEEDS	
WEED CONTROL	

WATER

WATER SCHEDULE	RAINFALL
MON TUES WED THUR FRI SAT SUN	MON TUES WED THUR FRI SAT SUN

OUTCOME

BLOOM	HARVEST

PLANT RATING 🌿 🌿 🌿 🌿 🌿

PLANT LOG

PLANT NAME		
SCIENTIFIC NAME		
SUPPLIER		COST

PLANT TYPE

☐ ANNUAL ☐ BIENNIAL ☐ BULB ☐ FLOWER ☐ FRUIT ☐ HERB
☐ PERENNIAL ☐ SEEDLING ☐ SHRUB ☐ SUCCULENT ☐ TRANSPLANT
☐ TREE ☐ VEGETABLE

PLANT DETAILS

DATE PLANTED	DATE GERMINATED	LOCATION	LIGHT CONDITIONS
			SUN ☐ PART SUN ☐ SHADE ☐

FERTILIZER	
SOIL AMENDMENTS	
PESTS	
PEST CONTROL	
WEEDS	
WEED CONTROL	

WATER

WATER SCHEDULE	RAINFALL
MON TUES WED THUR FRI SAT SUN	MON TUES WED THUR FRI SAT SUN

OUTCOME

BLOOM	HARVEST

PLANT RATING 🍃 🍃 🍃 🍃 🍃

PLANT LOG

PLANT NAME	
SCIENTIFIC NAME	
SUPPLIER	COST

PLANT TYPE

☐ ANNUAL ☐ BIENNIAL ☐ BULB ☐ FLOWER ☐ FRUIT ☐ HERB
☐ PERENNIAL ☐ SEEDLING ☐ SHRUB ☐ SUCCULENT ☐ TRANSPLANT
☐ TREE ☐ VEGETABLE

PLANT DETAILS

DATE PLANTED	DATE GERMINATED	LOCATION	LIGHT CONDITIONS
			SUN ☐ PART SUN ☐ SHADE ☐

FERTILIZER	
SOIL AMENDMENTS	
PESTS	
PEST CONTROL	
WEEDS	
WEED CONTROL	

WATER

WATER SCHEDULE	RAINFALL
MON TUES WED THUR FRI SAT SUN	MON TUES WED THUR FRI SAT SUN

OUTCOME

BLOOM	HARVEST

PLANT RATING 🌿🌿🌿🌿🌿

PLANT LOG

PLANT NAME	
SCIENTIFIC NAME	
SUPPLIER		COST	

PLANT TYPE

☐ ANNUAL ☐ BIENNIAL ☐ BULB ☐ FLOWER ☐ FRUIT ☐ HERB
☐ PERENNIAL ☐ SEEDLING ☐ SHRUB ☐ SUCCULENT ☐ TRANSPLANT
☐ TREE ☐ VEGETABLE

PLANT DETAILS

DATE PLANTED	DATE GERMINATED	LOCATION	LIGHT CONDITIONS
			SUN ☐ PART SUN ☐ SHADE ☐

FERTILIZER	
SOIL AMENDMENTS	
PESTS	
PEST CONTROL	
WEEDS	
WEED CONTROL	

WATER

WATER SCHEDULE	RAINFALL
MON TUES WED THUR FRI SAT SUN	MON TUES WED THUR FRI SAT SUN

OUTCOME

BLOOM	HARVEST

PLANT RATING 🍃🍃🍃🍃🍃

PLANT LOG

PLANT NAME	
SCIENTIFIC NAME	
SUPPLIER	COST

PLANT TYPE

- ☐ ANNUAL ☐ BIENNIAL ☐ BULB ☐ FLOWER ☐ FRUIT ☐ HERB
- ☐ PERENNIAL ☐ SEEDLING ☐ SHRUB ☐ SUCCULENT ☐ TRANSPLANT
- ☐ TREE ☐ VEGETABLE

PLANT DETAILS

DATE PLANTED	DATE GERMINATED	LOCATION	LIGHT CONDITIONS
			SUN ☐ PART SUN ☐ SHADE ☐

FERTILIZER	
SOIL AMENDMENTS	
PESTS	
PEST CONTROL	
WEEDS	
WEED CONTROL	

WATER

WATER SCHEDULE	RAINFALL
MON TUES WED THUR FRI SAT SUN	MON TUES WED THUR FRI SAT SUN

OUTCOME

BLOOM	HARVEST

PLANT RATING 🌿 🌿 🌿 🌿 🌿

PLANT LOG

PLANT NAME	
SCIENTIFIC NAME	
SUPPLIER	COST

PLANT TYPE

☐ ANNUAL ☐ BIENNIAL ☐ BULB ☐ FLOWER ☐ FRUIT ☐ HERB
☐ PERENNIAL ☐ SEEDLING ☐ SHRUB ☐ SUCCULENT ☐ TRANSPLANT
☐ TREE ☐ VEGETABLE

PLANT DETAILS

DATE PLANTED	DATE GERMINATED	LOCATION	LIGHT CONDITIONS
			SUN ☐ PART SUN ☐ SHADE ☐

FERTILIZER	
SOIL AMENDMENTS	
PESTS	
PEST CONTROL	
WEEDS	
WEED CONTROL	

WATER

WATER SCHEDULE	RAINFALL
MON TUES WED THUR FRI SAT SUN	MON TUES WED THUR FRI SAT SUN

OUTCOME

BLOOM	HARVEST

PLANT RATING 🍃🍃🍃🍃🍃

PLANT LOG

PLANT NAME	
SCIENTIFIC NAME	
SUPPLIER	COST

PLANT TYPE

- ☐ ANNUAL ☐ BIENNIAL ☐ BULB ☐ FLOWER ☐ FRUIT ☐ HERB
- ☐ PERENNIAL ☐ SEEDLING ☐ SHRUB ☐ SUCCULENT ☐ TRANSPLANT
- ☐ TREE ☐ VEGETABLE

PLANT DETAILS

DATE PLANTED	DATE GERMINATED	LOCATION	LIGHT CONDITIONS
			SUN ☐ PART SUN ☐ SHADE ☐

FERTILIZER	
SOIL AMENDMENTS	
PESTS	
PEST CONTROL	
WEEDS	
WEED CONTROL	

WATER

WATER SCHEDULE	RAINFALL
MON TUES WED THUR FRI SAT SUN	MON TUES WED THUR FRI SAT SUN

OUTCOME

BLOOM	HARVEST

PLANT RATING 🌿 🌿 🌿 🌿 🌿

PLANT LOG

PLANT NAME	
SCIENTIFIC NAME	
SUPPLIER	COST

PLANT TYPE

☐ ANNUAL ☐ BIENNIAL ☐ BULB ☐ FLOWER ☐ FRUIT ☐ HERB

☐ PERENNIAL ☐ SEEDLING ☐ SHRUB ☐ SUCCULENT ☐ TRANSPLANT

☐ TREE ☐ VEGETABLE

PLANT DETAILS

DATE PLANTED	DATE GERMINATED	LOCATION	LIGHT CONDITIONS
			SUN ☐ PART SUN ☐ SHADE ☐

FERTILIZER	
SOIL AMENDMENTS	
PESTS	
PEST CONTROL	
WEEDS	
WEED CONTROL	

WATER

WATER SCHEDULE	RAINFALL
MON TUES WED THUR FRI SAT SUN	MON TUES WED THUR FRI SAT SUN

OUTCOME

BLOOM	HARVEST

PLANT RATING 🌿 🌿 🌿 🌿 🌿

PLANT LOG

PLANT NAME	
SCIENTIFIC NAME	
SUPPLIER	COST

PLANT TYPE

- [ ] ANNUAL
- [ ] BIENNIAL
- [ ] BULB
- [ ] FLOWER
- [ ] FRUIT
- [ ] HERB
- [ ] PERENNIAL
- [ ] SEEDLING
- [ ] SHRUB
- [ ] SUCCULENT
- [ ] TRANSPLANT
- [ ] TREE
- [ ] VEGETABLE

PLANT DETAILS

DATE PLANTED	DATE GERMINATED	LOCATION	LIGHT CONDITIONS
			SUN ☐ PART SUN ☐ SHADE ☐

FERTILIZER	
SOIL AMENDMENTS	
PESTS	
PEST CONTROL	
WEEDS	
WEED CONTROL	

WATER

WATER SCHEDULE	RAINFALL
MON TUES WED THUR FRI SAT SUN	MON TUES WED THUR FRI SAT SUN

OUTCOME

BLOOM	HARVEST

PLANT RATING 🌿🌿🌿🌿🌿

PLANT LOG

PLANT NAME	
SCIENTIFIC NAME	

SUPPLIER		COST	

PLANT TYPE

- [ ] ANNUAL [ ] BIENNIAL [ ] BULB [ ] FLOWER [ ] FRUIT [ ] HERB
- [ ] PERENNIAL [ ] SEEDLING [ ] SHRUB [ ] SUCCULENT [ ] TRANSPLANT
- [ ] TREE [ ] VEGETABLE

PLANT DETAILS

DATE PLANTED	DATE GERMINATED	LOCATION	LIGHT CONDITIONS
			SUN [ ] PART SUN [ ] SHADE [ ]

FERTILIZER	
SOIL AMENDMENTS	
PESTS	
PEST CONTROL	
WEEDS	
WEED CONTROL	

WATER

WATER SCHEDULE	RAINFALL
MON TUES WED THUR FRI SAT SUN	MON TUES WED THUR FRI SAT SUN

OUTCOME

BLOOM	HARVEST

PLANT RATING 🍃 🍃 🍃 🍃 🍃

PLANT LOG

PLANT NAME	
SCIENTIFIC NAME	

SUPPLIER		COST	

PLANT TYPE

☐ ANNUAL ☐ BIENNIAL ☐ BULB ☐ FLOWER ☐ FRUIT ☐ HERB

☐ PERENNIAL ☐ SEEDLING ☐ SHRUB ☐ SUCCULENT ☐ TRANSPLANT

☐ TREE ☐ VEGETABLE

PLANT DETAILS

DATE PLANTED	DATE GERMINATED	LOCATION	LIGHT CONDITIONS
			SUN ☐ PART SUN ☐ SHADE ☐

FERTILIZER	
SOIL AMENDMENTS	
PESTS	
PEST CONTROL	
WEEDS	
WEED CONTROL	

WATER

WATER SCHEDULE	RAINFALL
MON TUES WED THUR FRI SAT SUN	MON TUES WED THUR FRI SAT SUN

OUTCOME

BLOOM	HARVEST

PLANT RATING 🍃🍃🍃🍃🍃

PLANT LOG

PLANT NAME	
SCIENTIFIC NAME	
SUPPLIER	COST

PLANT TYPE

☐ ANNUAL ☐ BIENNIAL ☐ BULB ☐ FLOWER ☐ FRUIT ☐ HERB
☐ PERENNIAL ☐ SEEDLING ☐ SHRUB ☐ SUCCULENT ☐ TRANSPLANT
☐ TREE ☐ VEGETABLE

PLANT DETAILS

DATE PLANTED	DATE GERMINATED	LOCATION	LIGHT CONDITIONS
			SUN ☐ PART SUN ☐ SHADE ☐

FERTILIZER	
SOIL AMENDMENTS	
PESTS	
PEST CONTROL	
WEEDS	
WEED CONTROL	

WATER

WATER SCHEDULE	RAINFALL
MON TUES WED THUR FRI SAT SUN	MON TUES WED THUR FRI SAT SUN

OUTCOME

BLOOM	HARVEST

PLANT RATING 🍃🍃🍃🍃🍃

PLANT LOG

PLANT NAME	
SCIENTIFIC NAME	

SUPPLIER		COST	

PLANT TYPE

- [ ] ANNUAL
- [ ] BIENNIAL
- [ ] BULB
- [ ] FLOWER
- [ ] FRUIT
- [ ] HERB
- [ ] PERENNIAL
- [ ] SEEDLING
- [ ] SHRUB
- [ ] SUCCULENT
- [ ] TRANSPLANT
- [ ] TREE
- [ ] VEGETABLE

PLANT DETAILS

DATE PLANTED	DATE GERMINATED	LOCATION	LIGHT CONDITIONS
			SUN ☐ PART SUN ☐ SHADE ☐

FERTILIZER	
SOIL AMENDMENTS	
PESTS	
PEST CONTROL	
WEEDS	
WEED CONTROL	

WATER

WATER SCHEDULE	RAINFALL
MON TUES WED THUR FRI SAT SUN	MON TUES WED THUR FRI SAT SUN

OUTCOME

BLOOM	HARVEST

PLANT RATING 🌿 🌿 🌿 🌿 🌿

PLANT LOG

PLANT NAME		
SCIENTIFIC NAME		
SUPPLIER		COST

PLANT TYPE

☐ ANNUAL ☐ BIENNIAL ☐ BULB ☐ FLOWER ☐ FRUIT ☐ HERB
☐ PERENNIAL ☐ SEEDLING ☐ SHRUB ☐ SUCCULENT ☐ TRANSPLANT
☐ TREE ☐ VEGETABLE

PLANT DETAILS

DATE PLANTED	DATE GERMINATED	LOCATION	LIGHT CONDITIONS
			SUN ☐ PART SUN ☐ SHADE ☐

FERTILIZER	
SOIL AMENDMENTS	
PESTS	
PEST CONTROL	
WEEDS	
WEED CONTROL	

WATER

WATER SCHEDULE	RAINFALL
MON TUES WED THUR FRI SAT SUN	MON TUES WED THUR FRI SAT SUN

OUTCOME

BLOOM	HARVEST

PLANT RATING ✿ ✿ ✿ ✿ ✿

PLANT LOG

PLANT NAME	
SCIENTIFIC NAME	
SUPPLIER	COST

PLANT TYPE

☐ ANNUAL ☐ BIENNIAL ☐ BULB ☐ FLOWER ☐ FRUIT ☐ HERB

☐ PERENNIAL ☐ SEEDLING ☐ SHRUB ☐ SUCCULENT ☐ TRANSPLANT

☐ TREE ☐ VEGETABLE

PLANT DETAILS

DATE PLANTED	DATE GERMINATED	LOCATION	LIGHT CONDITIONS
			SUN ☐ PART SUN ☐ SHADE ☐

FERTILIZER	
SOIL AMENDMENTS	
PESTS	
PEST CONTROL	
WEEDS	
WEED CONTROL	

WATER

WATER SCHEDULE	RAINFALL
MON TUES WED THUR FRI SAT SUN	MON TUES WED THUR FRI SAT SUN

OUTCOME

BLOOM	HARVEST

PLANT RATING 🍃 🍃 🍃 🍃 🍃

PLANT LOG

PLANT NAME	
SCIENTIFIC NAME	

SUPPLIER		COST	

PLANT TYPE

☐ ANNUAL ☐ BIENNIAL ☐ BULB ☐ FLOWER ☐ FRUIT ☐ HERB

☐ PERENNIAL ☐ SEEDLING ☐ SHRUB ☐ SUCCULENT ☐ TRANSPLANT

☐ TREE ☐ VEGETABLE

PLANT DETAILS

DATE PLANTED	DATE GERMINATED	LOCATION	LIGHT CONDITIONS
			SUN ☐ PART SUN ☐ SHADE ☐

FERTILIZER	
SOIL AMENDMENTS	
PESTS	
PEST CONTROL	
WEEDS	
WEED CONTROL	

WATER

WATER SCHEDULE	RAINFALL
MON TUES WED THUR FRI SAT SUN	MON TUES WED THUR FRI SAT SUN

OUTCOME

BLOOM	HARVEST

PLANT RATING 🍃 🍃 🍃 🍃 🍃

PLANT LOG

PLANT NAME	
SCIENTIFIC NAME	

SUPPLIER		COST	

PLANT TYPE

- [ ] ANNUAL
- [ ] BIENNIAL
- [ ] BULB
- [ ] FLOWER
- [ ] FRUIT
- [ ] HERB
- [ ] PERENNIAL
- [ ] SEEDLING
- [ ] SHRUB
- [ ] SUCCULENT
- [ ] TRANSPLANT
- [ ] TREE
- [ ] VEGETABLE

PLANT DETAILS

DATE PLANTED	DATE GERMINATED	LOCATION	LIGHT CONDITIONS
			SUN [ ] PART SUN [ ] SHADE [ ]

FERTILIZER	
SOIL AMENDMENTS	
PESTS	
PEST CONTROL	
WEEDS	
WEED CONTROL	

WATER

WATER SCHEDULE	RAINFALL
MON TUES WED THUR FRI SAT SUN	MON TUES WED THUR FRI SAT SUN

OUTCOME

BLOOM	HARVEST

PLANT RATING 🌿🌿🌿🌿🌿

PLANT LOG

PLANT NAME	
SCIENTIFIC NAME	
SUPPLIER	COST

PLANT TYPE

- [ ] ANNUAL [ ] BIENNIAL [ ] BULB [ ] FLOWER [ ] FRUIT [ ] HERB
- [ ] PERENNIAL [ ] SEEDLING [ ] SHRUB [ ] SUCCULENT [ ] TRANSPLANT
- [ ] TREE [ ] VEGETABLE

PLANT DETAILS

DATE PLANTED	DATE GERMINATED	LOCATION	LIGHT CONDITIONS
			SUN [ ] PART SUN [ ] SHADE [ ]

FERTILIZER	
SOIL AMENDMENTS	
PESTS	
PEST CONTROL	
WEEDS	
WEED CONTROL	

WATER

WATER SCHEDULE	RAINFALL
MON TUES WED THUR FRI SAT SUN	MON TUES WED THUR FRI SAT SUN

OUTCOME

BLOOM	HARVEST

PLANT RATING

PLANT LOG

PLANT NAME	
SCIENTIFIC NAME	

SUPPLIER		COST	

PLANT TYPE

- ☐ ANNUAL ☐ BIENNIAL ☐ BULB ☐ FLOWER ☐ FRUIT ☐ HERB
- ☐ PERENNIAL ☐ SEEDLING ☐ SHRUB ☐ SUCCULENT ☐ TRANSPLANT
- ☐ TREE ☐ VEGETABLE

PLANT DETAILS

DATE PLANTED	DATE GERMINATED	LOCATION	LIGHT CONDITIONS
			SUN ☐ PART SUN ☐ SHADE ☐

FERTILIZER	
SOIL AMENDMENTS	
PESTS	
PEST CONTROL	
WEEDS	
WEED CONTROL	

WATER

WATER SCHEDULE	RAINFALL
MON TUES WED THUR FRI SAT SUN	MON TUES WED THUR FRI SAT SUN

OUTCOME

BLOOM	HARVEST

PLANT RATING 🍃 🍃 🍃 🍃 🍃

PLANT LOG

PLANT NAME	
SCIENTIFIC NAME	
SUPPLIER	**COST**

PLANT TYPE

☐ ANNUAL   ☐ BIENNIAL   ☐ BULB   ☐ FLOWER   ☐ FRUIT   ☐ HERB

☐ PERENNIAL   ☐ SEEDLING   ☐ SHRUB   ☐ SUCCULENT   ☐ TRANSPLANT

☐ TREE   ☐ VEGETABLE

PLANT DETAILS

DATE PLANTED	DATE GERMINATED	LOCATION	LIGHT CONDITIONS
			SUN ☐ PART SUN ☐ SHADE ☐

FERTILIZER	
SOIL AMENDMENTS	
PESTS	
PEST CONTROL	
WEEDS	
WEED CONTROL	

WATER

WATER SCHEDULE	RAINFALL
MON TUES WED THUR FRI SAT SUN	MON TUES WED THUR FRI SAT SUN

OUTCOME

BLOOM	HARVEST

PLANT RATING 🌿 🌿 🌿 🌿 🌿

SEED INVENTORY

VARIETY	COMPANY	DATE PURCHASED	QUANTITY

SEED INVENTORY

VARIETY	COMPANY	DATE PURCHASED	QUANTITY

SEED INVENTORY

VARIETY	COMPANY	DATE PURCHASED	QUANTITY

TOOL INVENTORY

INVENTORY	INVENTORY

SUPPLIER LIST

SUPPLIER	PRODUCTS
COMPANY	
WEBSITE	
ADDRESS	
PHONE NUMBER	

SUPPLIER	PRODUCTS
COMPANY	
WEBSITE	
ADDRESS	
PHONE NUMBER	

SUPPLIER	PRODUCTS
COMPANY	
WEBSITE	
ADDRESS	
PHONE NUMBER	

SUPPLIER LIST

SUPPLIER	PRODUCTS
COMPANY	
WEBSITE	
ADDRESS	
PHONE NUMBER	

SUPPLIER	PRODUCTS
COMPANY	
WEBSITE	
ADDRESS	
PHONE NUMBER	

SUPPLIER	PRODUCTS
COMPANY	
WEBSITE	
ADDRESS	
PHONE NUMBER	

SUPPLIER LIST

SUPPLIER	PRODUCTS
COMPANY	
WEBSITE	
ADDRESS	
PHONE NUMBER	

SUPPLIER	PRODUCTS
COMPANY	
WEBSITE	
ADDRESS	
PHONE NUMBER	

SUPPLIER	PRODUCTS
COMPANY	
WEBSITE	
ADDRESS	
PHONE NUMBER	

SUPPLIER LIST

SUPPLIER	PRODUCTS
COMPANY	
WEBSITE	
ADDRESS	
PHONE NUMBER	

SUPPLIER	PRODUCTS
COMPANY	
WEBSITE	
ADDRESS	
PHONE NUMBER	

SUPPLIER	PRODUCTS
COMPANY	
WEBSITE	
ADDRESS	
PHONE NUMBER	

SUPPLIER LIST

SUPPLIER	PRODUCTS
COMPANY	
WEBSITE	
ADDRESS	
PHONE NUMBER	

SUPPLIER	PRODUCTS
COMPANY	
WEBSITE	
ADDRESS	
PHONE NUMBER	

SUPPLIER	PRODUCTS
COMPANY	
WEBSITE	
ADDRESS	
PHONE NUMBER	

SUPPLIER LIST

SUPPLIER	PRODUCTS
COMPANY	
WEBSITE	
ADDRESS	
PHONE NUMBER	

SUPPLIER	PRODUCTS
COMPANY	
WEBSITE	
ADDRESS	
PHONE NUMBER	

SUPPLIER	PRODUCTS
COMPANY	
WEBSITE	
ADDRESS	
PHONE NUMBER	

SUPPLIER LIST

SUPPLIER	PRODUCTS
COMPANY	
WEBSITE	
ADDRESS	
PHONE NUMBER	

SUPPLIER	PRODUCTS
COMPANY	
WEBSITE	
ADDRESS	
PHONE NUMBER	

SUPPLIER	PRODUCTS
COMPANY	
WEBSITE	
ADDRESS	
PHONE NUMBER	

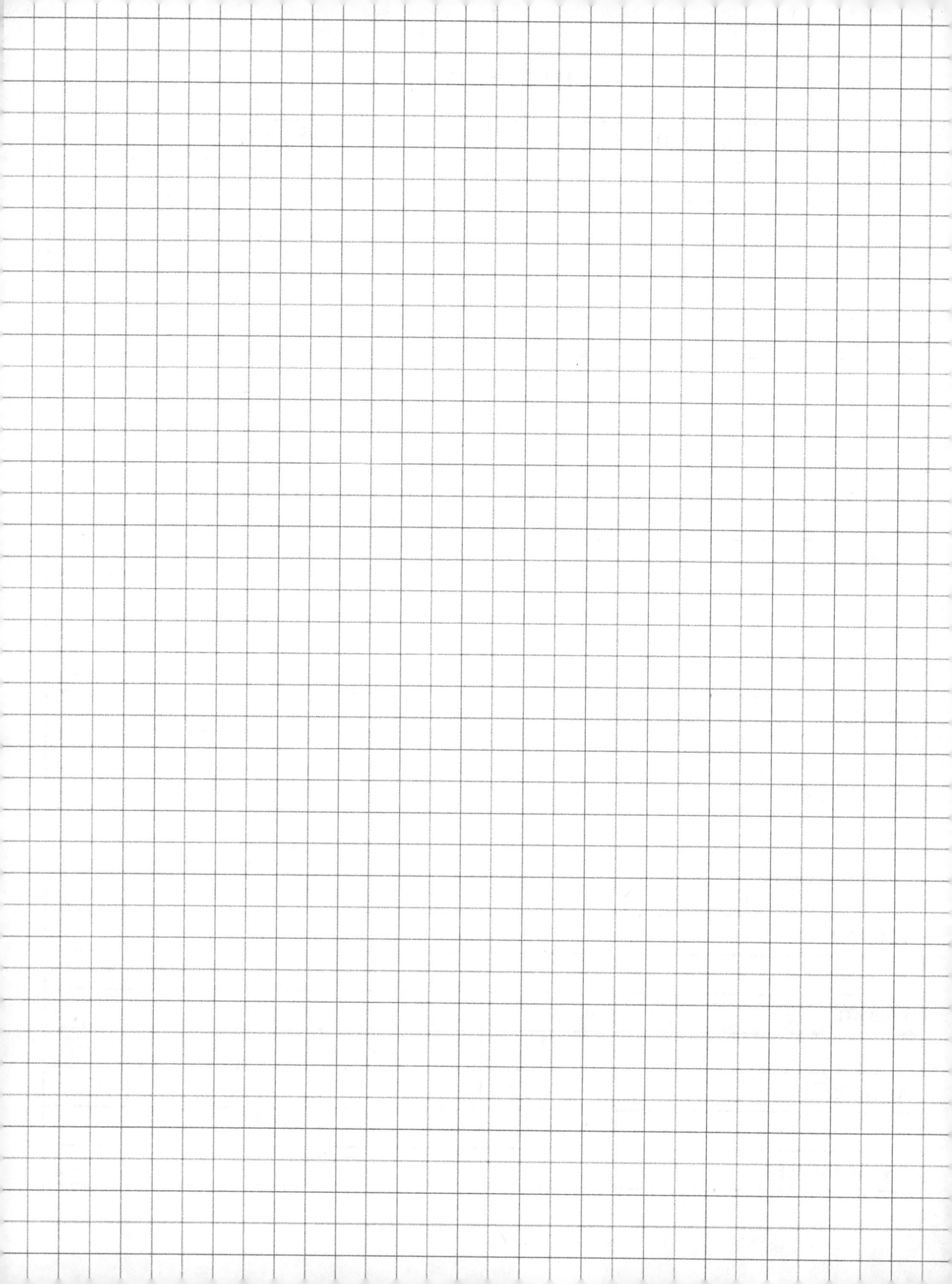

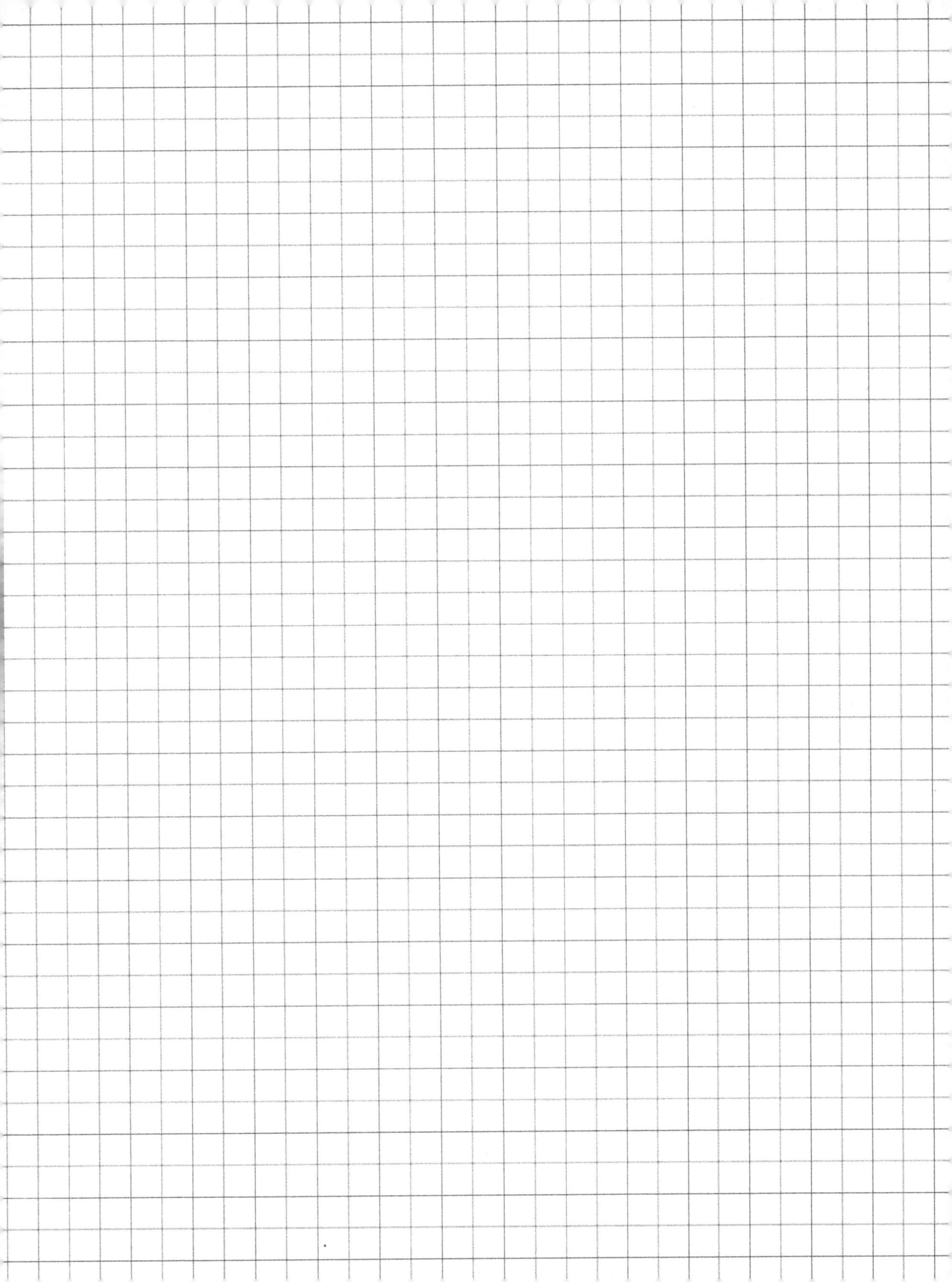

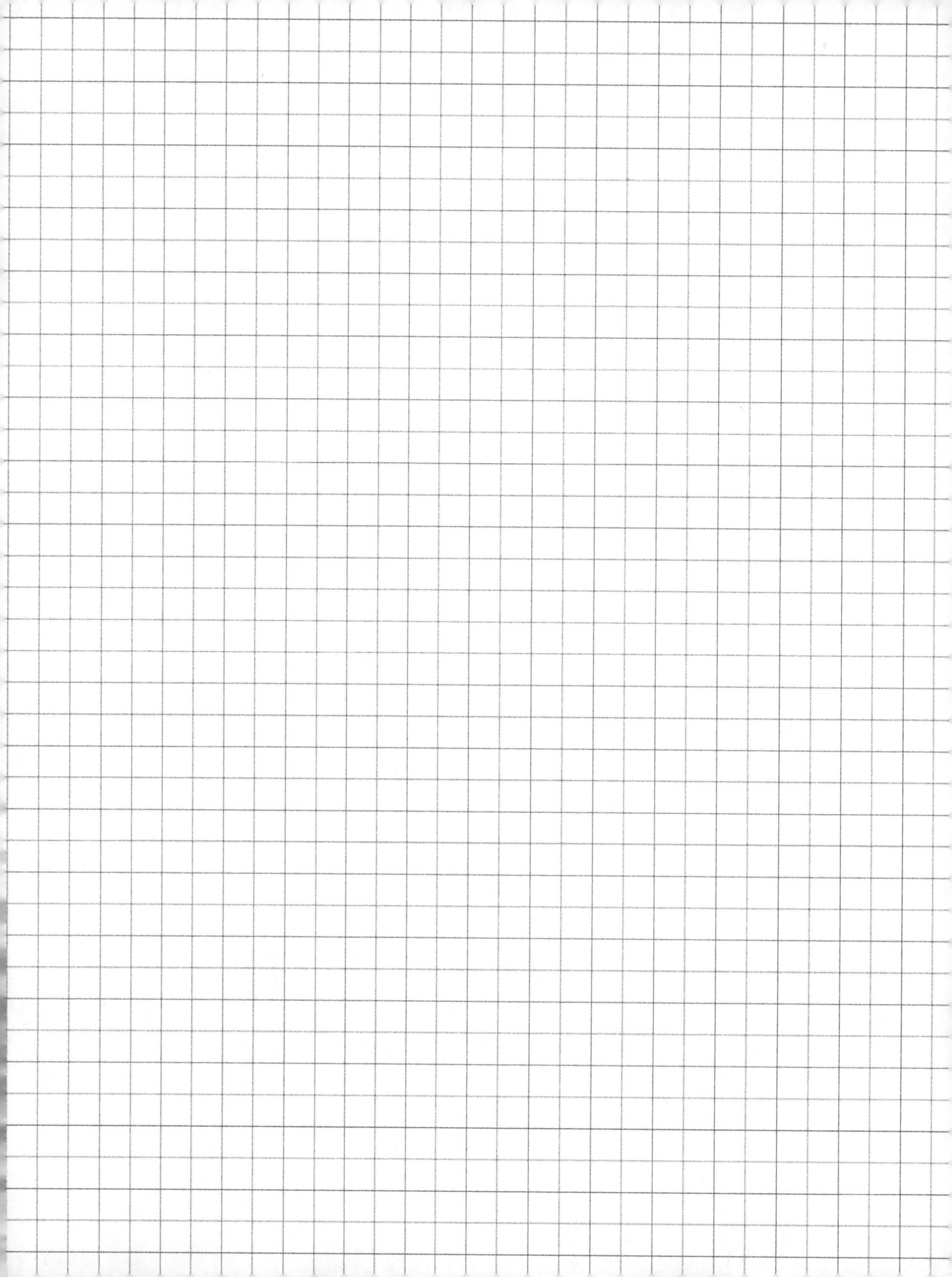

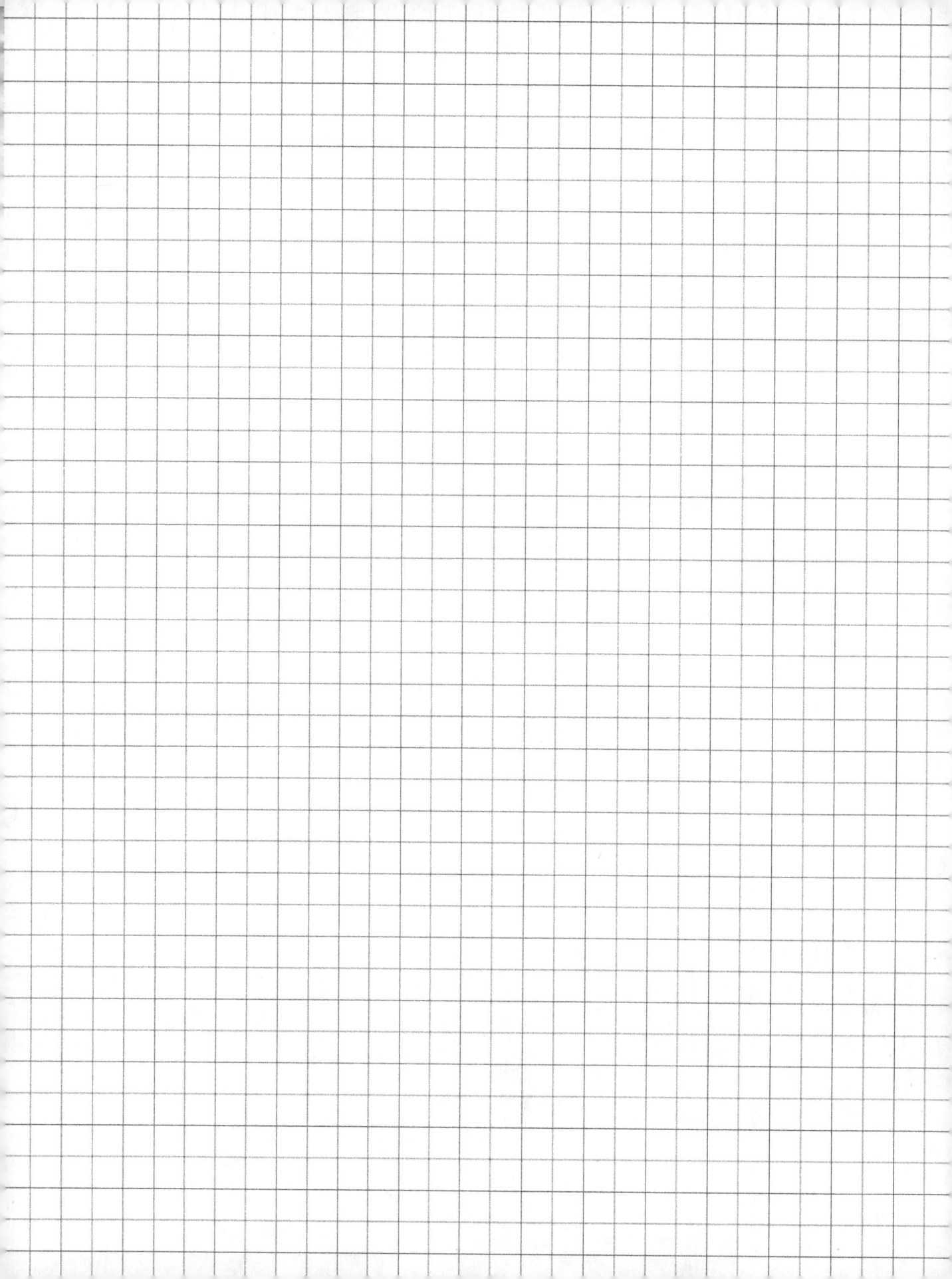

WISH LIST

MY WISH LIST

WISH LIST

MY WISH LIST